Power and Peace in Prayer

Power
and Peace in
Prayer

R. A. Torrey

GOOD NEWS PUBLISHERS
Westchester, Illinois 60153

This edition of
Power and Peace in Prayer
is abridged from the original edition of *How to Pray*
published by several publishers
in the United States and England.

A *One Evening Christian Classic*™
Copyright© 1978 Good News Publishers
Westchester, Illinois 60153
All rights reserved.
Printed in the United States of America
ISBN 0-89107-019-2

CONTENTS

POWER AND PEACE IN

Prayer

CHAPTER 1

THE IMPORTANCE OF PRAYER

>>>> With startling and overwhelming force the tre-
mendous importance of prayer is set forth in Ephesians
6:18: "Praying always with all prayer and supplication in
the Spirit, and watching thereunto with all perseverance
and supplication for all saints."

When we stop to weigh the meaning of these words,
then note the connection in which they are found, the in-
telligent child of God is driven to say, "I must pray, pray,
pray. I must put all my energy and all my heart into prayer.
Whatever else I do, I must pray."

The Revised Version is, if possible, stronger than the
Authorized: "With all prayer and supplication praying at
all seasons in the Spirit, and watching thereunto in all perseverance and supplication for all the saints."

Note the *alls*: "with *all* prayer," "at *all* seasons," "in
all perseverance," "for *all* the saints." Note the piling up of
strong words, "prayer," "supplication," "perseverance."
Note once more the strong expression, "watching thereunto," more literally, "being sleepless thereunto."
Paul realized the natural slothfulness of man, and especial-
ly his natural slothfulness in prayer. How seldom we pray
things through! How often the church and the individual
get right up to the verge of a great blessing in prayer and

just then let go, get drowsy and quit. I wish that these words "being sleepless unto prayer" might burn into our hearts. I wish the whole verse might burn into our hearts.

But why is this constant, persistent, sleepless, overcoming prayer so needful?

1. *Because there is a Devil.*

He is cunning, he is mighty, he never rests, he is ever plotting the downfall of the child of God; and if the child of God relaxes in prayer the Devil will succeed in ensnaring him.

This is the thought of the context. Verse 12 reads: "For our wrestling is not against flesh and blood, but against the principalities, against the powers, against the world rulers of this darkness, against the spiritual hosts of wickedness in the heavenly places" (R.V.). Then comes verse 13: "Wherefore take up the whole armor of God, that ye may be able to withstand in the evil day, and, having done all, to stand" (R.V.). Next follows a description of the different parts of the Christian's armor which we are to put on if we are to stand against the Devil and his mighty wiles. Then Paul brings all to a climax in verse 18, telling us that to all else we must add prayer—constant, persistent, untiring, sleepless prayer in the Holy Spirit or all else will go for nothing.

2. *Prayer is God's appointed way for obtaining things, and the great secret of all lack in our experience, in our life and in our work is neglect of prayer.*

James brings this out very forcibly in chapter 4 and verse 2 of his epistle: "Ye have not because ye ask not." These words contain the secret of the poverty and powerlessness of the average Christian—neglect of prayer.

Many a Christian is asking, "Why is it I make so little progress in my Christian life?"

"Neglect of prayer," God answers. "You have not because you ask not."

The belt of truth.
The breastplate of righteousness
feet fitted readiness from the gospel of peace
The shield of faith

helmet of salvation
sword of the Spirit which is the word of God

Many a minister is asking, "Why is it I see so little fruit from my labors?"

Again God answers, "Neglect of prayer. You have not because you ask not."

Many a Sunday school teacher is asking, "Why is it that I see so few converted in my Sunday school class?"

Still God answers, "Neglect of prayer. You have not because you ask not."

Both ministers and churches are asking, "Why is it that the church of Christ makes so little headway against unbelief and error and sin and worldliness?"

Once more we hear God answering, "Neglect of prayer. You have not because you ask not."

3.   *Those men whom God set forth as a pattern of what He expected Christians to be—the apostles—regarded prayer as the most important business of their lives.*

When the multiplying responsibilities of the Early Church crowded in upon them, they "called the multitude of the disciples unto them, and said, It is not reason that we should leave the Word of God, and serve tables. Wherefore, brethren, look ye out among you seven men of honest report, full of the Holy Ghost and wisdom, whom we may appoint over this business. But *we will give ourselves continually to prayer* and to the ministry of the Word." It is evident from what Paul wrote to the churches and to individuals about praying for them that much of his time and strength and thought were given to prayer (Rom. 1:9, R. V.; Eph. 1:15, 16; Col. 1:9, R. V.; I Thess. 3:10; II Tim. 1:3, R.V.)

All the mighty men of God outside the Bible have been men of prayer. They have differed from one another in many things but in this they have been alike.

4.   *Prayer occupied a very prominent place and played a very important part in the earthly life of our Lord.*

Turn, for example, to Mark 1:35. "And in the morning, rising up a great while before day, he went out, and departed into a solitary place, and there prayed." The preceding day had been a very busy and exciting one but Jesus shortened the hours of needed sleep that He might arise early and give Himself to more sorely needed prayer.

Turn again to Luke 6:12, where we read, "And it came to pass in those days that he went out into a mountain to pray, and continued all night in prayer to God." Our Saviour found it necessary on occasion to take a whole night for prayer.

The words *pray* and *prayer* are used at least twenty-five times in connection with our Lord in the brief record of His life in the four Gospels, and His praying is mentioned in places where the words are not used. Evidently prayer took much of the time and strength of Jesus; a man or woman who does not spend much time in prayer cannot properly be called a follower of Jesus Christ.

5. *Praying is the most important part of the present ministry of our risen Lord.* This reason for constant, persistent, sleepless, overcoming prayer seems if possible even more forcible.

Christ's ministry did not close with His death. His atoning work was finished then, but when He rose and ascended to the right hand of the Father He entered upon other work for us just as important in its place as His atoning work. It cannot be divorced from His atoning work; it rests upon that as its basis but it is necessary to our complete salvation.

What that great present work is, by which He carries our salvation on to completeness, we read in Hebrews 7:25: "Wherefore he is able also to save them to the uttermost that come unto God by him, seeing *he ever liveth to make intercession for them.*" This verse tells us that Jesus is able to save us unto the uttermost, not merely *from* the uttermost, but *unto* the uttermost, unto entire completeness. He did not merely die but He also "ever liveth."

The verse also tells us for what purpose He now lives, *"to make intercession for us,"* to pray. Praying is the principal thing He is doing in these days. It is by His prayers that He is saving us.

The same thought is found in Paul's remarkable triumphant challenge in Romans 8:34: "Who is he that shall condemn? It is Christ Jesus that died, yea rather, that was raised from the dead, who is at the right hand of God, *who also maketh intercession for us"* (R. V.)

If we then are to have fellowship with Jesus Christ in His present work we must spend much time in prayer; we must give ourselves to earnest, constant, persistent, sleepless, overcoming prayer. I know of nothing that has so impressed me with a sense of the importance of praying at all seasons, being much and constantly in prayer, as the thought that that is the principal occupation at present of my risen Lord. I want to have fellowship with Him and to that end I have asked the Father whatever else He may make me to make me at all events an intercessor, to make me a man who knows how to pray and who spends much time in prayer.

This ministry of intercession is a glorious and a mighty ministry and we can all have part in it. The man or the woman who is shut away from the public meeting by sickness can have part in it; the busy mother; the widow who has to earn her own living can have part; the hard-driven man of business can have part in it, praying as he hurries from duty to duty. But of course we must, if we would maintain this spirit of constant prayer, take time—and take plenty of it—when we shall shut ourselves up in the secret place alone with God for nothing but prayer.

6.   *Prayer is the means that God has appointed for our receiving mercy and obtaining grace to help in time of need.*

Hebrews 4:16 is one of the simplest and sweetest verses in the Bible, "Let us therefore come boldly unto the throne of grace, that we may obtain mercy, and find grace to help in time of need." These words make it very plain that God has appointed a way by which we shall seek and obtain mercy and grace. That way is prayer; bold, confident, outspoken approach to the throne of grace, the most holy place of God's presence, where our sympathizing High Priest, Jesus Christ, has entered in our behalf (vv. 14, 15).

Mercy is what we need, grace is what we must have, or all our life and effort will end in complete failure. Prayer is the way to get them. There is infinite grace at our disposal and we make it ours experimentally by prayer. Oh, if we only realized the fullness of God's grace that is ours for the asking, its height and depth and length and breadth, I am sure that we would spend more time in prayer. The measure of our appropriation of grace is determined by the measure of our prayers.

Who is there that does not feel that he needs more grace? Then ask for it. Be constant and persistent in your asking. Be importunate and untiring in your asking. God delights to have us "shameless" beggars in this direction; for it shows our faith in Him and He is mightily pleased with faith. Because of our "shamelessness" He will rise and give us as much as we need (Luke 11:8). What little streams of mercy and grace most of us know when we might know rivers overflowing their banks!

7.   *Prayer in the name of Jesus Christ is the way Jesus Christ Himself has appointed for His disciples to obtain fullness of joy.*

He states this simply and beautifully in John 16:24: "Hitherto have ye asked nothing in my name; ask, and ye shall receive, that your joy may be fulfilled." "Made full" is the way the Revised Version reads. Who is there that does not wish his joy filled full? Well, the way to have it filled full is by praying in the name of Jesus. We all know people whose joy is filled full; indeed, it is just running over, shining from their eyes; bubbling out of their lips and running off their fingertips when they shake hands with you. Coming in contact with them is like coming in contact with an electrical machine charged with gladness. Now people of that sort are always people that spend much time in prayer.

Why is it that prayer in the name of Christ brings such fullness of joy? In part, because we get what we ask. But that is not the only reason nor the greatest. It makes God real. When we ask something definite of God, and He gives it, how real God becomes! He is right there! It is blessed to have a God who is real and not merely an idea. I remember how once I was taken suddenly and seriously sick all alone in my study. I dropped upon my knees and cried to God for help. Instantly all pain left me—I was perfectly well. It seemed as if God stood right there and had put out His hand and touched me. The joy of the healing was not so great as the joy of meeting God.

There is no greater joy on earth or in Heaven than communion with God and prayer in the name of Jesus brings us into communion with Him. The Psalmist was surely not speaking only of future blessedness but also of present blessedness when he said, "In thy presence is fullness of joy" (Ps. 16:11). Oh, the unutterable joy of those moments when in our prayers we really press into the presence of God!

Does someone say, "I have never known any such joy as that in prayer"?

Do you take enough leisure for prayer to actually get into God's presence? Do you really give yourself up to prayer in the time which you do take?

8. Prayer in every care and anxiety and need of

life, with thanksgiving, is the means that God has appointed for our obtaining freedom from all anxiety, and the peace of God which passeth all understanding.

"Be careful for nothing," says Paul, "but in everything by prayer and supplication with thanksgiving let your requests be made known unto God, and the peace of God which passeth all understanding, shall keep your hearts and minds through Christ Jesus" (Phil. 4:6, 7). To many this seems at the first glance the picture of a life that is beautiful but beyond the reach of ordinary mortals; not so at all. The verse tells us how the life is attainable by every child of God: "Be careful for nothing," or as the Revised Version reads, "In nothing be anxious." The remainder of the verse tells us how and it is very simple: "But in everything by prayer and supplication with thanksgiving let your requests be made known unto God." What could be plainer or more simple than that? Just keep in constant touch with God and when any trouble or vexation, great or small, comes up, speak to Him about it, never forgetting to return thanks for what He has already done. What will the result be? "The peace of God which passeth all understanding shall guard your hearts and your thoughts in Christ Jesus" (R. V.).

That is glorious and as simple as it is glorious! Thank God, many are trying it. Don't you know anyone who is always serene? Perhaps he is a very stormy man by his natural make-up but troubles and conflicts and reverses and bereavements may sweep around him and the peace of God which passes all understanding guards his heart and his thoughts in Christ Jesus.

We all know such persons. How do they manage it?

Just by prayer. That is all. Those persons who know the deep peace of God, the unfathomable peace that passes all understanding, are always men and women of much prayer.

Some of us let the hurry of our lives crowd prayer out and what a waste of time and energy and nerve force there is by the constant worry! One night of prayer will save us from many nights of insomnia. Time spent in prayer is not wasted but time invested at big interest.

9.   *Prayer is the means that Christ has appointed whereby our hearts shall not become over-charged with surfeiting and drunkenness and cares of this life, and so the day of Christ's return come upon us suddenly.*

One of the most interesting and solemn passages upon prayer in the Bible is along this line (Luke 21:34-36). "Take heed to yourselves, lest at any time your hearts be overcharged with surfeiting and drunkenness and cares of this life, and so that day come upon you unawares. For as a snare shall it come on all them that dwell on the face of the whole earth. Watch ye therefore, and *pray always,* that ye may be accounted worthy to escape all these things that shall come to pass, and to stand before the Son of man." According to this passage there is only one way in which we can be prepared for the coming of the Lord when He appears; that is through much prayer.

The coming again of Jesus Christ is a subject that is awakening much interest and much discussion in our day; but it is one thing to be interested in the Lord's return and to talk about it and quite another thing to be prepared for it. We live in an atmosphere that has a constant tendency to unfit us for Christ's coming. The world tends to draw us down by its materialism and by its cares. There is only one way by which we can rise triumphant above these things—by constant watching unto prayer. *Watch* in this passage is the same strong word used in Ephesians 6:18, and *always* the same strong phrase *in every season.* The man who spends little time in prayer, who is not steadfast and constant in prayer, will not be ready for the Lord when He comes. But we may be ready. How? Pray! Pray! Pray!

10. *Because of what prayer accomplishes.* Much has really been said upon that already but there is much also that should be added.

(a) *Prayer promotes our spiritual growth* as almost nothing else, indeed as nothing else but Bible study; and true prayer and true Bible study go hand in hand.

It is through prayer that my sin is brought to light, my most hidden sin. As I kneel before God and pray, "Search me, O God, and know my heart: try me, and know my thoughts: and see if there be any wicked way in me" (Ps. 139:23, 24), God shoots the penetrating rays of His light into the innermost recesses of my heart and the sins I never suspected are brought to view. In answer to prayer God washes me from my iniquity and cleanses me from my sin (Psa. 51:2). In answer to prayer my eyes are opened to behold wondrous things out of God's Word (Psa. 119:18). In answer to prayer I get wisdom to know God's way (James 1:5) and strength to walk in it. As I meet God in prayer and gaze into His face I am changed into His own image from glory to glory (II Cor. 3:18). Each day of true prayer life finds me more like my glorious Lord.

(b) *Prayer brings power into our work.* If we wish power for any work to which God calls us, be it preaching, teaching, personal work, or the rearing of our children, we can get it by earnest prayer.

A woman with a little boy who was perfectly incorrigible once came to me in desperation and said:

"What shall I do with him?"

I asked, "Have you ever tried prayer?"

She said that she had prayed for him she thought. I asked if she had made his conversion and his character a matter of definite, expectant prayer. She replied that she had not been definite in the matter. She began that day. At once there was a marked change in the child and he grew up into Christian manhood.

How many a Sunday school teacher has taught for months and years, and seen no real fruit from his labors. Then he has learned the secret of intercession and by earnest pleading with God has seen his scholars brought one by one to Christ! How many a poor preacher has become a mighty man of God by casting away his confidence in his own ability and gifts and giving himself up to God to wait upon Him for the power that comes from on high! John Livingstone spent a night in prayer to God. When he preached next day in the Kirk of Shotts five hundred people were converted or dated some definite uplift in their life to that occasion. Prayer and power are inseparable.

(c)   *Prayer avails for the conversion of others.* There are few converted in this world unless in connection with someone's prayers. I formerly thought that no human being had anything to do with my own conversion for I was not converted in church or Sunday school or in personal conversation with anyone. I was awakened in the middle of the night and converted. As far as I can remember I had not the slightest thought of being converted when I went to bed and fell asleep; but I was awakened in the middle of the night and converted probably inside of five minutes. A few minutes before I was about as near eternal perdition as one gets. I had one foot over the brink and was trying to get the other one over. I say I thought no human being had anything to do with it but I had forgotten my mother's prayers. I afterwards learned that one of my college classmates had chosen me as one to pray for until I was saved.

Prayer often avails where everything else fails. How utterly all of Monica's efforts and entreaties failed with her son! But her prayers prevailed with God and the dissolute youth became St. Augustine, the mighty man of God. By prayer the bitterest enemies of the gospel have become its most valiant defenders, the greatest scoundrels the truest sons of God, and the vilest women the purest saints. Oh, the power of prayer to reach down, down, down where hope itself seems vain and lift men and women up, up, up into fellowship with and likeness to God! It is simply wonderful! How little we appreciate this marvelous weapon!

(d)   *Prayer brings blessings to the Church*. The history of the Church has always been a history of grave difficulties to overcome. The Devil hates the Church and seeks in every way to block its progress; now by false doctrine, again by division, again by inward corruption of life. But by prayer a clear way can be made through everything. Prayer will root out heresy, allay misunderstanding, sweep away jealousies and animosities, obliterate immoralities and bring in the full tide of God's reviving grace. History abundantly proves this. In the hour of darkest portent, when the case of the Church, local or universal, has seemed beyond hope, believing men and believing women have met together and cried to God and the answer has come.

It was so in the days of Knox, it was so in the days of Wesley and Whitefield, it was so in the days of Finney. And it will be so again in your day! Satan has marshalled his forces. The world, the flesh and the Devil are holding high carnival. It is now a dark day, *but*—now "it is time for thee, Lord, to work; for they have made void thy law" (Psa. 119:126). He is getting ready to work. Now He is listening for the voice of prayer. Will He hear it? Will He hear it from you? Will He hear it from the Church as a body? I believe He will.

CHAPTER 2

PRAYING TO GOD

>>>> We have seen something of the tremendous importance and the resistless power of prayer. Now we come directly to the theme—how to pray with power.

1.   In the twelfth chapter of the Acts of the Apostles we have the record of a prayer that prevailed with God and brought to pass great results. In the fifth verse of this chapter, the manner and method of this prayer is described in few words:

"Prayer was made without ceasing of the church *unto God* for him."

The first thing to notice in this verse is the brief expression "unto God." The prayer that has power is the prayer that is offered unto God.

But some will say, "Is not all prayer unto God?"

No. Very much of so-called prayer, both public and private, is not unto God. In order that a prayer should be really unto God there must be a definite and conscious approach to God when we pray. We must have a definite and vivid realization that God is bending over us and listening as we pray. In very much of our prayer there is really but little thought of God. Our mind is taken up with the thought of what we need and is not occupied with the thought of the mighty and loving Father of whom we are seeking it. Oftentimes it is the case that we are occupied neither with the need nor with the One to whom we are praying but our mind is wandering here and there throughout the world. There is no power in that sort of prayer. But when we really come into God's presence, really meet Him face to face in the place of prayer, really seek the things that we desire *from Him,* then there is power.

If, then, we would pray aright, the first thing that we should do is to see that we really get an audience with God, that we really get into His very presence. Before a word of petition is offered we should have the definite and vivid consciousness that we are talking to God and should believe that He is listening to our petition and is going to grant the thing that we ask of Him. This is possible only by the Holy Spirit's power, so we should look to the Holy Spirit to really lead us into the presence of God and should not be hasty in words until He has actually brought us there.

One night a very active Christian man dropped into a little prayer meeting that I was leading. Before we knelt to pray I said something like the above, telling all the friends to be sure before they prayed, and while they were praying, that they really were in God's presence, that they had the thought of Him definitely in mind, and to be more taken up with Him than with their petition. A few days after I met this same gentleman and he said that this simple thought was entirely new to him, that it had made prayer an entirely new experience to him.

If then we would pray aright these two little words must sink deep into our heart, *unto God.*

2.   The second secret of effective praying is found in the same verse, in the words, *without ceasing.*

In the Revised Version, "without ceasing" is rendered "earnestly." Neither rendering gives the full force of the Greek. The word means literally "stretched-out-ed-ly." It is a pictorial word and wonderfully expressive. It represents the soul on a stretch of earnest and intense desire. "Intensely" would perhaps come as near translating it as any English word. It is the word used of our Lord in Luke 22:44 where it is said, "He prayed more earnestly, and his sweat was as it were great drops of blood falling down to the ground."

We read in Hebrews 5:7 that "in the days of his flesh" Christ "offered up prayers and supplications with strong crying and tears." In Romans 15:30 Paul beseeches the saints in Rome to *strive* together with him in their prayers. The word translated *strive* means primarily to contend as in athletic games or in a fight. In other words the prayer that prevails with God is the prayer into which we put our whole soul, stretching out toward God in intense and agonizing desire. Much of our modern prayer has no power in it because there is no heart in it. We rush into God's presence, run through a string of petitions, jump up and go out. If someone should ask us an hour afterward for what we prayed, oftentimes we could not tell. If we put so little heart into our prayers we cannot expect God to put much heart into answering them.

When we learn to come to God with an intensity of desire that wrings the soul, then shall we know a power in prayer that most of us do not know now.

But how shall we attain to this earnestness in prayer?

Not by trying to work ourselves up into it. The true method is explained in Romans 8:26: "And in like manner the Spirit also helpeth our infirmity: for we know not how to pray as we ought; but the Spirit himself maketh intercession for us with groanings which cannot be uttered" (R. V.). The earnestness that we work up in the energy of the flesh is a repulsive thing. The earnestness wrought in us by the Holy Spirit is pleasing to God. Here again, if we would pray aright, we must look to the Spirit of God to teach us to pray.

It is in this connection that fasting comes. In Daniel

9:3 we read that Daniel set his face "unto the Lord God, to seek by prayer and supplications, with fasting, and sackcloth, and ashes." There are those who think that fasting belongs to the old dispensation; but when we look at Acts 14:23 and Acts 13:2, 3, we find that it was practiced by the earnest men of the apostolic day.

If we would pray with power, we should pray with fasting. This of course does not mean that we should fast every time we pray; but there are times of emergency or special crisis in work or in our individual lives, when men of downright earnestness will withdraw themselves even from the gratification of natural appetites that would be perfectly proper under other circumstances that they may give themselves up wholly to prayer. There is a peculiar power in such prayer. Every great crisis in life and work should be met in that way. There is nothing pleasing to God in our giving up in a purely Pharisaic and legal way things which are pleasant but there is power in that downright earnestness and determination to obtain in prayer the things of which we sorely feel our need that leads us to put away everything, even things in themselves most right and necessary, that we may set our faces to find God and obtain blessings from Him.

3.   A third secret of right praying is also found in this same verse, Acts 12:5. It appears in the three words, *of the church.*

There is power in *united prayer.* Of course there is power in the prayer of an individual but there is vastly increased power in united prayer. God delights in the unity of His people and seeks to emphasize it in every way. So He pronounces a special blessing upon united prayer. We read in Matthew 18:19, "If two of you shall agree on earth as touching anything that they shall ask, it shall be done for them of my Father which is in heaven." This unity, however, must be real. The passage just quoted does not say that if two shall agree in asking, but if two shall agree *as touching* anything they shall ask. Two persons might agree to ask for the same thing and yet there be no real agreement as touching the thing they asked. One might ask it because he really desired it, the other might ask it simply to please his friend. But where there is real agreement, where the Spirit of God brings two believers into perfect harmony as concerning that which they may ask of God, where the Spirit lays the same burden on two hearts, in all such prayer there is absolutely irresistible power.

CHAPTER 3

OBEYING AND PRAYING

➤➤➤➤ 1.   One of the most significant verses in the Bible on prayer is I John 3:22. John says, "And whatsoever we ask, we receive of him, because we keep his commandments and do those things that are pleasing in his sight."

What an astounding statement! John says in so many words that everything he asked for he got. How many of us can say this: "Whatsoever I ask I receive"? But John explains why this was so, "Because we keep his commandments, and do those things that are pleasing in his sight." In other words, the one who expects God to do as he asks Him must on his part *do whatever God bids him.* If we give a listening ear to all God's commands to us He will give a listening ear to all our petitions to Him. If, on the other hand, we turn a deaf ear to His precepts He will be likely to turn a deaf ear to our prayers. Here we find the secret of much unanswered prayer. We are not listening to God's Word and therefore He is not listening to our petitions.

I was once speaking to a woman who had been a professed Christian but had given it all up. I asked her why she was not a Christian still. She replied because she did not believe the Bible. I asked her why she did not believe the Bible.

"Because I have tried its promises and found them untrue."

"Which promises?"

"The promises about prayer."

"Which promises about prayer?"

"Does it not say in the Bible, 'Whatsoever ye ask believing ye shall receive?' "

"It says something nearly like that."

"Well, I asked fully expecting to get and did not receive, so the promise failed."

"Was the promise made to you?"

"Why, certainly, it is made to all Christians, is it not?"

"No, God carefully defines who the *ye's* are whose believing prayers He agrees to answer."

I then turned her to I John 3:22 and read the description of those who prayers had power with God.

"Now," I said, "were you keeping His commandments and doing those things which are pleasing in His sight?"

She frankly confessed that she was not and soon came to see that the real difficulty was not with God's promises but with herself. That is the difficulty with many an unanswered prayer today: the one who offers it is not obedient.

If we would have power in prayer we must be earnest students of His Word to find out what His will regarding us is, and then having found it do it. One unconfessed act of disobedience on our part will shut the ear of God against many petitions.

2.   But this verse goes beyond the mere keeping of God's commandments. John tells us that we must *do those things that are pleasing in His sight.*

There are many things which it would be pleasing to God for us to do which He has not specifically commanded us. A true child is not content with merely doing those things which his father specifically commands him to do. He studies to know his father's will and if he thinks that there is any thing that he can do that would please his father he does it gladly, though his father has never given him any specific order to do it. So it is with the true child of God. He does not ask merely whether certain things are commanded or certain things forbidden. He studies to know his Father's will in all things.

There are many Christians today who are doing things that are not pleasing to God and leaving undone things which would be pleasing to God. When you speak to them about these things they will confront you at once with the question, "Is there any command in the Bible not to do this thing?" And if you cannot show them the verse in which the matter in question is plainly forbidden they think they are under no obligation whatever to give it up; but a true child of God does not demand a specific command. If we make it our study to find out and do the things which are pleasing to God, He will make it His study to do the things which are pleasing to us. Here again we find the explanation of much unanswered prayer: We are not making it the study of our lives to know what would please our Father and so our prayers are not answered.

Take as an illustration of questions that are constant-ly coming up, the matter of theater-going, dancing and the use of tobacco. Many who are indulging in these things will ask you triumphantly if you speak against them, "Does the Bible say, 'Thou shalt not go to the theater'?" "Does the Bible say, 'Thou shalt not dance'?" "Does the Bible say, 'Thou shalt not smoke'?" That is not the ques-tion. The question is, Is our heavenly Father well pleased when He sees one of His children in the theater, at the dance, or smoking? That is a question for each to decide for himself, prayerfully, seeking light from the Holy Spirit. "Where is the harm in these things?" many ask. It is aside from our purpose to go into the general question but be-yond a doubt there is great harm in many a case; they rob our prayers of power.

3. Psalm 145:18 throws a great deal of light on the question of how to pray: "The Lord is nigh unto all them that call upon him, to all that call upon him in truth."

That little expression *in truth* is worthy of study. If you will take your concordance and go through the Bible you will find that this expression means "in reality," "in sincerity." The prayer that God answers is the prayer that is real, the prayer that asks for something that is sin-cerely desired.

Much prayer is insincere. People ask for things which they do not wish. Many a woman is praying for the con-version of her husband who does not really wish her hus-band to be converted. She thinks that she does. But if she knew what would be involved in the conversion of her husband, how it would necessitate an entire revolution in his manner of doing business, and how consequently it would reduce their income and make necessary an en-tire change in their method of living, the real prayer of her heart would be, if she were to be sincere with God:

"O God, do not convert my husband."

She does not wish his conversion at so great cost.

Many a church is praying for a revival that does not really desire a revival. They think they do, for to their minds a revival means an increase of membership, an increase of income, an increase of reputation among the churches; but if they knew what a real revival meant, what a searching of hearts on the part of professed Christians would be involved, what a radical transformation of individual, domestic and social life would be brought about, and many other things that would come to pass if the Spirit of God was poured out in reality and power; if all this were known the real cry of the church would be:

"O God, keep us from having a revival."

Many a minister is praying for the filling with the Holy Spirit who does not really desire it. He thinks he does, for the filling with the Spirit means to him new joy, new power in preaching the Word, a wider reputation among men, a larger prominence in the church of Christ. But if he understood what a filling with the Holy Spirit really involved, how for example it would necessarily bring him into antagonism with the world, and with unspiritual Christians, how it would cause his name to be "cast out as evil," how it might necessitate his leaving a good comfortable living and going down to work in the slums, or even in some foreign land; if he understood all this, his prayer quite likely would be—if he were to express the real wish of his heart—"O God, save me from being filled with the Holy Ghost."

But when we do come to the place where we really desire the conversion of friends at any cost, really desire the outpouring of the Holy Spirit whatever it may involve, where we desire anything "in truth" and then call upon God for it "in truth," God is going to hear.

CHAPTER 4

PRAYING IN THE NAME OF CHRIST AND ACCORDING TO THE WILL OF GOD

>>>> 1.   It was a wonderful word about prayer that Jesus spoke to His disciples on the night before His crucifixion: "Whatsoever ye shall ask *in my name,* that will I do, that the Father may be glorified in the Son. If ye shall ask anything in my name, I will do it."

Prayer in the name of Christ has power with God. God is well pleased with His Son Jesus Christ. He hears Him always, and He also hears always the prayer that is really in His name. There is a fragrance in the name of Christ that makes acceptable to God every prayer that bears it.

But what is it to pray in the name of Christ?

Many explanations have been attempted that to ordinary minds do not explain. But there is nothing mystical or mysterious about this expression. If one will go through the Bible and examine all the passages in which the expression "in my name" or "in his name" or synonymous expressions are used he will find that it means just about what it does in modern usage. If I go to a bank and hand in a check with my name signed to it I ask of that bank *in my own name.* If I have money deposited in that bank the check will be cashed; if not, it will not be. If, however, I go to a bank with somebody's else name signed to the check I am asking *in his name* and it does not matter whether I have money in that bank or any other, if the person whose name is signed to the check has money there the check will be cashed.

If, for example, I should go to the First National Bank of Chicago, and present a check which I had signed for $50.00, the paying teller would say to me:

"Why, Mr. Torrey, we cannot cash that. You have no money in this bank."

But if I should go to the First National Bank with a check for $50.00 made payable to me and signed by one of the large depositors in that bank, they would not ask whether I had money in that bank or in any bank but would honor the check at once.

It is like going to the bank of Heaven when I go to God in prayer. I have nothing deposited there; I have absolutely no credit there. If I go in my own name I will get absolutely nothing; but Jesus Christ has unlimited credit in Heaven and He has granted to me the privilege of going to the bank with His name on my checks. When I thus go my prayers will be honored to any extent.

To pray then in the name of Christ is to pray on the ground not of my credit but His; to renounce the thought that I have any claims on God whatever and approach Him on the ground of Christ's claims. Praying in the name of Christ is not merely adding the phrase, "I ask these things in Jesus' name," to my prayer. I may put that phrase in my prayer and really be resting in my own merit all the time. On the other hand I may omit that phrase but really be resting in the merit of Christ all the time. But when I really do approach God, not on the ground of my merit, but on the ground of Christ's merit, not on the ground of my goodness, but on the ground of the atoning blood (Heb. 10:19), God will hear me. Very much of our modern prayer is vain because men approach God imagining that they have some claim upon God whereby He is ander obligation to answer their prayers.

Years ago when Mr. Moody was young in Christian

work, he visited a town in Illinois. A judge in the town
was an infidel. This judge's wife besought Mr. Moody to
call upon her husband, but Mr. Moody replied:

"I cannot talk with your husband. I am only an un-
educated young Christian and your husband is a book
infidel."

But the wife would not take *no* for an answer so Mr.
Moody made the call. The clerks in the outer office tittered
as the young salesman from Chicago went in to talk
with the scholarly judge.

The conversation was short. Mr. Moody said:

"Judge, I can't talk with you. You are a book infidel
and I have no learning. But I simply want to say if you are
ever converted I want you to let me know."

The judge replied: "Yes, young man, if I am ever
converted I will let you know. Yes, I will let you know."

The conversation ended. The clerks tittered still louder
when the zealous young Christian left the office but the
judge was converted within a year. Mr. Moody visiting the
town again asked the judge to explain how it came about.
The judge said:

"One night when my wife was at prayer meeting I
began to grow very uneasy and miserable. I did not know
what was the matter with me but finally retired before my
wife came home. I could not sleep all that night. I got up
early, told my wife that I would eat no breakfast, and
went down to the office. I told the clerks they could take
a holiday and shut myself up in the inner office. I kept
growing more and more miserable and finally I got down
and asked God to forgive my sins. But I would not say
'for Jesus' sake' for I was a Unitarian and I did not believe
in the atonement. I kept praying 'God forgive my sins'; but
no answer came. At last in desperation I cried, 'O God,

for Christ's sake forgive my sins,' and found peace at once."

The judge had no access to God until he came in the name of Christ, but when he thus came he was heard and answered at once.

2.   Great light is thrown upon the subject "How to Pray" by I John 5:14, 15: "And this is the boldness which we have toward him, that if we ask anything *according to his will,* he heareth us: and if we know that he heareth us whatsoever we ask, we know that we have the petitions which we have asked of him" (R. V.).

This passage teaches us plainly that if we are to pray aright we must pray according to God's will, then will we beyond a peradventure get the thing we ask of Him.

But can we know the will of God? Can we know that any specific prayer is according to His will?

We most surely can.

How?

(a)   First by the Word. God has revealed His will in His Word. When anything is definitely promised in the Word of God we know that it is His will to give that thing. If then when I pray I can find some definite promise of God's Word and lay that promise before God I know that He hears me, and if I know that He hears me I know that I have the petition that I have asked of Him. For example, when I pray for wisdom I know that it is the will of God to give me wisdom for He says so in James 1:5: "If any of you lack wisdom, let him ask of God, that giveth to all men liberally, and upbraideth not; and it shall be given him." So when I ask for wisdom I know that the prayer is heard and that wisdom will be given me.

Some years ago a minister came to me at the close of an address on prayer at a YMCA Bible school and said,

"You have produced upon those young men the impression that they can ask for definite things and get the very things that they ask."

I replied that I did not know whether that was the impression that I had produced or not but that was certainly the impression that I desired to produce.

"But," he replied, "that is not right. We cannot be sure for we don't know God's will."

I turned him at once to James 1:5, read it and said to him, "Is it not God's will to give us wisdom, and if you ask for wisdom do you not know that you are going to get it?"

"Ah!" he said, "we don't know what wisdom is."

I said, "No, if we did, we would not need to ask; but whatever wisdom may be don't you know that you will get it?"

Here is one of the greatest secrets of prevailing prayer: To study the Word to find what God's will is as revealed there in the promises and then simply take these promises and spread them out before God in prayer with the absolutely unwavering expectation that He will do what He has promised in His Word.

(b)   But there is still another way in which we may know the will of God; that is by the teaching of His Holy Spirit. There are many things that we need from God which are not covered by any specific promise, but we are not left in ignorance of the will of God even then. In Romans 8:26, 27 we were told, "And in like manner the Spirit also helpeth our infirmity: for we know not how to pray as we ought; but the Spirit himself maketh intercession for us with groanings which cannot be uttered; and he that searcheth the hearts knoweth what is the mind of the Spirit, because he maketh intercession for the saints

according to the will of God" (R. V.) Here we are distinct-
ly told that the Spirit of God prays in us, draws out our
prayer, in the line of God's will. When we are thus led
out by the Holy Spirit in any direction to pray for any given
object we may do it in all confidence that it is God's will
and that we are to get the very thing we ask of Him, even
though there is no specific promise to cover the case.
Often God by His Spirit lays upon us a heavy burden of
prayer for some given individual. We cannot rest, we
pray for him with groanings which cannot be uttered.
Perhaps the man is entirely beyond our reach but God
hears the prayer and in many a case it is not long before
we hear of his definite conversion.

The passage I John 5:14, 15, is one of the most abused
passages in the Bible: "This is *the confidence* that we have
in him, that, if we ask anything according to his will, he
heareth us; and if we know that he hear us, whatsoever
we ask, we know that we have the petitions that we desired
of him." The Holy Spirit beyond a doubt put it into the
Bible to encourage our faith. It begins with "This is *the*
confidence that we have in him" and closes with *"We*
know that we have the petitions that we desired of him";
but one of the most frequent usages of this passage which
was so manifestly given to beget confidence is to introduce
an element of uncertainty into our prayers. Oftentimes
when one waxes confident in prayer some cautious brother
will come and say:

"Now, don't be too confident. If it is God's will He
will do it. You should put in, 'If it be Thy will.' "

Doubtless there are many times when we do not know
the will of God and in all prayer submission to the excel-
lent will of God should underlie it; but when we know
God's will there need be no *if*'s; and this passage was not
put into the Bible in order that we might introduce *if*'s

into all our prayers but in order that we might throw our *if*'s to the wind and have *"confidence"* and *"know* that we have the petitions which we have asked of him."

CHAPTER 5

PRAYING IN THE SPIRIT

➤➤➤➤ 1. Over and over again in what has already been said, we have seen our dependence upon the Holy Spirit in prayer. This comes out very definitely in Ephesians 6:18, "Praying always with all prayer and supplication *in the Spirit"*, and in Jude 20, "Praying *in the Holy Ghost."* Indeed the whole secret of prayer is found in these three words, *in the Spirit*. It is the prayer that God the Holy Spirit inspires that God the Father answers.

The disciples did not know how to pray as they ought so they came to Jesus and said, "Lord, teach us to pray." We know not how to pray as we ought but we have another Teacher and Guide right at hand to help us (John 14:16, 17). "The Spirit helpeth our infirmity" (Rom. 8:26, R. V.). He teaches us how to pray. True prayer is prayer in the Spirit; that is, the prayer the Spirit inspires and directs. When we come into God's presence we should recognize "our infirmity," our ignorance of what we should pray for or how we should pray for it, and in the consciousness of our utter inability to pray aright we should look up to the Holy Spirit, casting ourselves utterly upon Him to direct our prayers, to lead out our desires and to guide our utterance of them.

When we first come into God's presence we should be silent before Him. We should look up to Him for His

Holy Spirit to teach us how to pray. We must surrender ourselves to the Spirit, then we shall pray aright.

Oftentimes when we come to God in prayer we do not feel like praying. What shall one do in such a case? Cease praying until he does feel like it? Not at all. When we feel least like praying is the time when we most need to pray. We should wait quietly before God and tell Him how cold and prayerless our hearts are, and look up to Him and trust Him and expect Him to direct the Holy Spirit to warm our hearts and draw them out in prayer. It will not be long before the glow of the Spirit's presence will fill our hearts and we will begin to pray with freedom, directness, earnestness and power. Many of the most blessed seasons of prayer I have ever known have begun with a feeling of utter deadness and prayerlessness; but in my helplessness and coldness I have cast myself upon God, and looked to His Holy Spirit to teach me to pray, and He has done it.

When we pray in the Spirit, we will pray for the right things and in the right way. There will be joy and power and peace in our prayer.

2.   If we are to pray with power we must pray *with faith*. In Mark 11:24 Jesus says, "Therefore I say unto you, What things soever ye desire, when ye pray, believe that ye receive them, and ye shall have them." No matter how positive any promise of God's Word may be we will not enjoy it in actual experience unless we confidently expect its fulfillment in answer to our prayer "If any of you lack wisdom," says James, "let him ask of God that giveth to all men liberally, and upbraideth not; and it shall be given him." Now that promise is as positive as a promise can be; but the next verse adds, "But let him ask in faith, nothing doubting: for he that doubteth is like the surge of the sea driven by the wind and tossed. For let not that man think that he shall receive anything of the Lord." (R. V.) There must then be confident, unwavering

expectation. But there is a faith that goes beyond expectation, that believes that the prayer is heard and the promise granted. This comes out in the Revised Version of Mark 11:24, "Therefore I say unto you, All things whatsoever ye pray and ask for, believe that ye *have* received them, and ye shall have them."

But how can one get this faith?

Let us say with all emphasis it cannot be pumped up. Many a one reads this promise about the prayer of faith and then asks for things that he desires and tries to make himself believe that God has heard the prayer. This ends only in disappointment for it is not real faith and the thing is not granted. It is at this point that many people make a collapse of faith altogether by trying to work up faith by an effort of their will.

Romans 10:17 answers the question: "So then faith cometh by hearing, and hearing *by the Word of God.*" If we are to have real faith, we must study the Word of God and find out what is promised, then simply believe the promises of God. Faith must have a warrant. Trying to believe something that you want to believe is not faith. Believing what God says in His Word is faith. If I am to have faith when I pray I must find some promise in the Word of God on which to rest my faith.

Faith furthermore comes through the Spirit. The Spirit knows the will of God. If I pray in the Spirit and look to the Spirit to teach me God's will He will lead me out in prayer along the line of that will and give me faith that the prayer is to be answered. But in no case does real faith come by simply determining that you are going to get the thing that you want to get. If there is no promise in the Word of God and no clear leading of the Spirit there can be no real faith, and there should be no upbraiding of self for lack of faith in such a case. But if the thing

desired is promised in the Word of God we may well up-
braid ourselves for lack of faith if we doubt, for we are
making God a liar by doubting His Word.

CHAPTER 6

ALWAYS PRAYING AND NOT FAINTING

➤➤➤➤ In two parables in the Gospel of Luke, Jesus
teaches with great emphasis the lesson that men ought always to pray and not to faint. The first parable is found
in Luke 11:5-8, and the other in Luke 18:1-8.

"And he said unto them, Which of you shall have
a friend, and shall go unto him at midnight, and say unto
him, Friend, lend me three loaves for a friend of mine
in his journey is come to me, and I have nothing to set
before him; and he from within shall answer and say,
Trouble me not: the door is now shut, and my children are
with me in bed. I cannot rise and give thee. I say unto
you, Though he will not rise and give him because he is
his friend, yet because of his importunity he will rise and
give him as many as he needeth" (Luke 11:5-8).

"And he spake a parable unto them to this end that
men ought always to pray and not to faint; saying, There
was in a city a judge which feared not God, neither regarded man; and there was a widow in that city; and she
came to him, saying,

"Avenge me of mine adversary.

"And he would not for a while: but afterward he said
within himself: 'Though I fear not God, nor regard man;
yet because this widow troubleth me, I will avenge

her, lest by her continual coming she weary me.

"And the Lord said, Hear what the unjust judge saith. And shall not God avenge his own elect, which cry day and night unto him, though he bear long with them? I tell you that he will avenge them speedily. Nevertheless when the Son of man cometh, shall he find faith on the earth?" (Luke 18:1-8).

In the former of these two parables Jesus sets forth the necessity of importunity in prayer in a startling way. The word rendered *importunity* means literally *shamelessness,* as if Jesus would have us understand that God would have us draw nigh to Him with a determination to obtain the things we seek that will not be put to shame by any seeming refusal or delay on God's part. God delights in the holy boldness that will not take *no* for an answer. It is an expression of great faith and nothing pleases God more than faith.

Jesus seemed to put the Syro-Phoenician woman away almost with rudeness; but she would not be put away, and Jesus looked upon her shameless importunity with pleasure and said, "O woman, great is thy faith: be it unto thee even as thou wilt" (Matt. 15:28). God does not always let us get things at our first effort. He would train us and make us strong men by compelling us to work hard for the best things. So also He does not always give us what we ask in answer to the first prayer; He would train us and make us strong men of prayer by compelling us to pray hard for the best things. He makes us *pray through.*

I am glad that this is so. There is no more blessed training in prayer than that that comes through being compelled to ask again and again and again even through a long period of years before one obtains that which he seeks from God. Many people call it submission to the will of

God when God does not grant them their requests at the first or second asking, and they say,

"Well, perhaps it is not God's will."

As a rule this is not submission but spiritual laziness. We do not call it submission to the will of God when we give up after one of two efforts to obtain things by action; we call it lack of strength of character. When the strong man of action starts out to accomplish a thing, if he does not accomplish it the first or second or one-hundredth time he keeps hammering away until he does accomplish it; and the strong man of prayer when he starts to pray for a thing keeps on praying until he prays it through and obtains what he seeks. We should be careful about what we ask from God but when we do begin to pray for a thing we should never give up praying for it until we get it or until God makes it very clear and very definite to us that it is not His will to give it.

Some would have us believe that it shows unbelief to pray twice for the same thing, that we ought to "take it" the first time that we ask. Doubtless there are times when we are able through faith in the Word or the leading of the Holy Spirit to *claim* the first time that which we have asked of God; but beyond question there are other times when we must pray again and again and again for the same thing before we get our answer. Those who have gotten beyond praying twice for the same thing have gotten beyond their Master (Matt. 26:44). George Mueller prayed for two men daily for upwards of sixty years. One of these men was converted shortly before his death, I think at the last service that George Mueller held; the other was converted within a year after his death. One of the great needs of the present day is men and women who will not only start out to pray for things but pray on and on and on until they obtain that which they seek from the Lord.

CHAPTER 7

ABIDING IN CHRIST

→→→→ "If ye abide in me and my words abide in you, ye shall ask what ye will, and it shall be done unto you" (John 15:7). The whole secret of prayer is found in these words of our Lord. Here is prayer that has unbounded power: "Ask *what ye will,* and it shall be done unto you."

There is a way then of asking and getting precisely what we ask and getting all we ask. Christ gives two conditions of this all-prevailing prayer:

1. The first condition is, "If ye abide in me."

What is it to abide in Christ?

Some explanations that have been given of this are so mystical or so profound that to many simple-minded children of God they mean practically nothing at all; but what Jesus meant was really very simple.

He had been comparing Himself to a vine, His disciples to the branches in the vine. Some branches continued in the vine; that is, remained in living union with the vine so that the sap or life of the vine constantly flowed into these branches. They had no independent life of their own. Everything in them was simply the outcome of the life of the vine flowing into them. Their buds, their leaves, their blossoms, their fruit, were really not theirs, but the buds, leaves, blossoms and fruit of the vine. Other branches were completely severed from the vine or else the flow of the sap of life of the vine into them was in some way hindered. Now for us to abide in Christ is for us to bear the same relation to Him that the first sort of branches bear to the vine; that is to say, to abide in Christ is to renounce any independent life of our own, to give up trying to think our thoughts or form our resolutions or cultivate our feelings, and simply and constantly look to Christ to think His thoughts in us, to form His purposes in us, to feel His emotions and affections in us. It is to renounce all life independent of Christ and constantly to look to Him for the inflow of His life into us and the outworking of His life through us. When we do this, and in so far as we do this, our prayers will obtain that which we seek from God.

This must necessarily be so, for our desires will not be our own desires but Christ's; our prayers will not in reality be our own prayers but Christ praying in us. Such prayers will always be in harmony with God's will and the Father heareth Him always. When our prayers fail it is because they are indeed our prayers. We have conceived the desire and framed the petition of ourselves instead of looking to Christ to pray through us.

To say that one should be abiding in Christ in all his prayers, looking to Christ to pray through Him rather than praying himself, is simply saying in another way that one should pray "in the Spirit." When we thus abide in Christ our thoughts are not our own thoughts but His; our joys are not our own joys but His; our fruit is not our own fruit but His; just as the buds, leaves, blossoms and fruit of the branch that abides in the vine are not the buds, leaves, blossoms and fruit of the branch but of the vine itself whose life is flowing into the branch.

To abide in Christ one must of course already be in Christ through the acceptance of Christ as an atoning Saviour from the guilt of sin, a risen Saviour from the power of sin, and a Lord and Master over all his life. Being in Christ, all that we have to do to abide (or continue) in

Christ is simply to renounce our self-life—utterly renouncing every thought, every purpose, every desire, every affection of our own and just looking day by day and hour by hour for Jesus Christ to form His thoughts, His purposes, His affections, His desires in us. Abiding in Christ is really a very simple matter though it is a wonderful life of privilege and of power.

2. But there is another condition stated in this verse, though it is really involved in the first: "And my words abide in you."

If we are to obtain from God all that we ask from Him, Christ's words must abide or continue in us. We must study His words, fairly devour His words, let them sink into our thought and into our heart, keep them in our memory, obey them constantly in our life, let them shape and mold our daily life and our every act.

This is really the method of abiding in Christ. It is through His words that Jesus imparts Himself to us. The words He speaks unto us, they are spirit and they are life (John 6:63). It is vain to expect power in prayer unless we meditate much upon the words of Christ and let them sink deep and find a permanent abode in our hearts. There are many who wonder why they are so powerless in prayer but the very simple explanation of it all is found in their neglect of the words of Christ. They have not hidden His words in their hearts; His words do not abide in them. It is not by seasons of mystical meditation and rapturous experiences that we learn to abide in Christ; it is by feeding upon His word, His written word as found in the Bible, and looking to the Holy Spirit to implant these words in our hearts and to make them a living thing in our hearts. If we thus let the words of Christ abide in us they will stir us up to prayer. They will be the mold in which our prayers are shaped and our prayers will be necessarily along the line of God's will and will prevail with Him. Prevailing prayer is almost an impossibility where there is neglect of the study of the Word of God.

Mere intellectual study of the Word of God is not enough; there must be meditation upon it. The Word of God must be revolved over and over and over in the mind, with a constant looking to God by His Spirit to make that Word a living thing in the heart. The prayer that is born of meditation upon the Word of God is the prayer that soars upward most easily to God's listening ear.

George Mueller, one of the mightiest men of prayer in past generations, when the hour for prayer came would begin by reading and meditating upon God's Word until out of the study of the Word a prayer began to form itself in his heart. Thus God Himself was the real author of the prayer and God answered the prayer which He Himself had inspired.

The one who would pray in the Spirit must meditate much upon the Word. If we would feed the fire of our prayers with the fuel of God's Word, all our difficulties in prayer would disappear.

CHAPTER 8

PRAYING WITH THANKSGIVING

>>>> There are two words often overlooked in the lesson about prayer which Paul gives us in Philippians 4:6, 7: "In nothing be anxious; but in everything by prayer and supplication with thanksgiving let your requests be made known unto God. And the peace of God, which passeth all understanding, shall guard your hearts and your thoughts in Christ Jesus" (R. V.) The two important words often overlooked are *with thanksgiving*.

In approaching God to ask for new blessings we should never forget to return thanks for blessings already granted. If any one of us would stop and think how many of the prayers which we have offered to God have been answered, and how seldom we have gone back to God to return thanks for the answers thus given, I am sure we would be overwhelmed with confusion. We should be just as definite in returning thanks as we are in prayer. We come to God with most specific petitions but when we return thanks to Him our thanksgiving is indefinite and general.

Doubtless one reason why so many of our prayers lack power is because we have neglected to return thanks for blessings already received. If anyone were to constantly come to us asking help from us and should never say "Thank you" for the help thus given we would soon tire of helping one so ungrateful. Indeed, regard for the one we were helping would hold us back from encouraging such rank ingratitude. Doubtless our heavenly Father out of a wise regard for our highest welfare oftentimes refuses to answer petitions that we send up to Him in order that we may be brought to a sense of our ingratitude and taught to be thankful.

God is deeply grieved by the thanklessness and ingratitude of which so many of us are guilty. When Jesus healed the ten lepers and only one came back to give Him thanks, in wonderment and pain He exclaimed, "Were not the ten cleansed? but where are the nine?" (Luke 17: 17, R. V.).

How often must He look down upon us in sadness at our forgetfulness of His repeated blessings and His frequent answer to our prayers.

Returning thanks for blessings already received increases our faith and enables us to approach God with new boldness and new assurance. Doubtless the reason so many have so little faith when they pray is because they take so little time to meditate upon and thank God for blessings already received. As one meditates upon the answers to prayers already granted faith waxes bolder and bolder and we come to feel in the very depths of our souls that there is nothing too hard for the Lord. As we reflect upon the wondrous goodness of God toward us on the one hand, and upon the other hand upon the little thought and strength and time that we ever put into thanksgiving, we may well humble ourselves before God and confess our sin.

The mighty men of prayer in the Bible and the mighty men of prayer throughout the ages of the church's history have been men who were much given to thanksgiving and praise. David was a mighty man of prayer, and how his Psalms abound with thanksgiving and praise. The apostles were mighty men of prayer; of them we read that "they were continually in the temple, praising and blessing God." Paul was a mighty man of prayer and how often in his epistles he bursts out in definite thanksgiving to God for definite blessings and definite answers to prayers. Jesus is our model in prayer as in everything else. We find in the study of His life that His manner of returning thanks at the simplest meal was so noticeable that two of His disciples recognized Him by this after His resurrection.

Thanksgiving is one of the inevitable results of being filled with the Holy Spirit and one who does not learn "in everything to give thanks" cannot continue to pray in the Spirit. If we would learn to pray with power we would do well to let these two words sink deep into our hearts: *"With thanksgiving."*

CHAPTER 9

HINDRANCES TO PRAYER

>>>> We have gone very carefully into the positive conditions of prevailing prayer; but there are some things which hinder prayer. These God has made very plain in His Word.

1.   The first hindrance to prayer we will find in James 4:3, "Ye ask and receive not *because ye ask amiss, that ye may spend it in your pleasures*" (R.V.).

A selfish purpose in prayer robs prayer of power. Very many prayers are selfish. These may be prayers for things for which it is perfectly proper to ask, for things which it is the will of God to give, but the motive of the prayer is entirely wrong and so the prayer falls powerless to the ground. The true purpose in prayer is that God may be glorified in the answer. If we ask any petition merely that we may receive something to use in our pleasures or in our own gratification in one way or another, we "ask amiss" and need not expect to receive what we ask. This explains why many prayers remain unanswered.

For example, many a woman is praying for the conversion of her husband. That certainly is a most proper thing to ask; but many a woman's motive in asking for the conversion of her husband is entirely selfish. She desires that her husband may be converted because it would be so much more pleasant for her to have a husband who sympathized with her. For some such selfish reason as this she desires to have her husband converted. Why should a woman desire the conversion of her husband? First of all and above all that God may be glorified; because she cannot bear the thought that God the Father should be dishonored by her husband trampling under foot the Son of God.

Many pray for a revival. That certainly is a prayer that is pleasing to God; it is along the line of His will; but many prayers for revivals are purely selfish. The churches desire revivals in order that the membership may be increased, in order that the church may have a position of more power and influence in the community, in order that the church treasury may be filled, in order that a good report may be made at the presbytery or conference or association. For such low purposes as these churches and ministers oftentimes are praying for a revival and oftentimes too God does not answer the prayer. Why should we pray for a revival? For the glory of God, because we cannot endure it that God should continue to be dishonored by the worldliness of the church, by the sins of unbelievers, by the proud unbelief of the day; because God's Word is being made void; in order that God may be glorified by the outpouring of His Spirit on the Church of Christ. For these reasons first of all and above all we should pray for a revival.

2.   The second hindrance to prayer we find in Isaiah 59:1, 2: "Behold, the Lord's hand is not shortened, that it cannot save; neither his ear heavy, that it cannot hear. But *your iniquities have separated between you and your God, and your sins have hid his face from you, that he will not hear.*"

Sin hinders prayer. Many a man prays and prays and prays and gets absolutely no answer to his prayer. Perhaps he is tempted to think that it is not the will of God to answer or he may think that the days when God answered prayer, if He ever did, are over. So the Israelites seem to have thought. They thought that the Lord's hand was shortened that it could not save and that His ear had become heavy that it could no longer hear.

"Not so," said Isaiah, "God's ear is just as open to hear as ever, His hand just as mighty to save; but there is a hindrance. That hindrance is your own sins. Your iniquities have separated between you and your God, and your sins have hid His face from you that He will not hear."

It is so today. Many and many a man is crying to God in vain simply because of sin in his life. It may be some sin in the past that has been unconfessed and unjudged, it may be some sin in the present that is cherished, very likely is not even looked upon as sin; but there the sin is, hidden away somewhere in the heart or in the life and God "will not hear."

Anyone who finds his prayers ineffective should not conclude that the thing which he asks of God is not according to His will but should go alone with God with the Psalmist's prayer, "Search me, O God, and know my heart: try me, and know my thoughts: and see if there be any wicked way in me" (Ps. 139:23, 24), and wait before Him until He puts His finger upon the thing that is displeasing in His sight. Then this sin should be confessed and put away.

I well remember a time in my life when I was praying for two definite things that it seemed that I must have or God would be dishonored; but the answer did not come. I awoke in the middle of the night in great physical suffering and great distress of soul. I cried to God for these things, reasoned with Him as to how necessary it was that I get them, and get them at once; but no answer came. I asked God to show me if there was anything wrong in my own life. Something came to my mind that had often come to it before, something definite but which I was unwilling to confess as sin. I said to God, "If this is wrong I will give it up"; but still no answer came. In my innermost heart, though I had never admitted it, I knew it was wrong.

At last I said:

"This is wrong. I have sinned. I will give it up."

I found peace. In a few moments I was sleeping like a child. In the morning I woke well in body and the money that was so much needed for the honor of God's name came.

Sin is an awful thing and one of the most awful things about it is the way it hinders prayer, the way it severs the connection between us and the source of all grace and power and blessing. Anyone who would have power in prayer must be merciless in dealing with his own sins. "If I regard iniquity in my heart, the Lord will not hear me" (Ps. 66:18). So long as we hold on to sin or have any controversy with God we cannot expect Him to heed our prayers. If there is anything that is constantly coming up in your moments of close communion with God that is the things that hinders prayer: put it away.

3.   The third hindrance to prayer is found in Ezekiel 14:3, "Son of man, these men have taken their idols into their heart, and put the stumbling block of their iniquity before their face: should I be inquired of at all by them?" (R. V.) *Idols in the heart cause God to refuse to listen to our prayers.*

What is an idol? An idol is anything that takes the place of God, anything that is the supreme object of our affection. God alone has the right to the supreme place in our hearts. Everything and everyone else must be subordinate to Him.

Many a man makes an idol of his wife. Not that a

man can love his wife any too much but he can put her in the wrong place; he can put her before God; and when a man regards his wife's pleasure before God's pleasure, when he gives her the first place and God the second place, his wife is an idol and God cannot hear his prayers.

Many a woman makes an idol of her children. Not that we can love our children too much. The more dearly we love Christ the more dearly we love our children; but we can put our children in the wrong place, we can put them before God, and their interests before God's interests. When we do this our children are our idols.

Many a man makes an idol of his reputation or his business. Reputation or business is put before God. God cannot hear the prayers of such a man.

One great question for us to decide if we would have power in prayer is, Is God absolutely first? Is He before wife, before children, before reputation, before business, before our own lives? If not, prevailing prayer is impossible.

God often calls our attention to the fact that we have an idol by not answering our prayers and thus leading us to inquire as to why our prayers are not answered; and so we discover the idol, put it away and God hears our prayers.

4.   The fourth hindrance to prayer is found in Proverbs 21:13, *"Whoso stoppeth his ears at the cry of the poor,* he also shall cry himself, but shall not be heard."

There is perhaps no greater hindrance to prayer than stinginess, the lack of liberality toward the poor and toward God's work. It is the one who gives generously to others who receives generously from God. "Give, and it shall be given unto you; good measure pressed down, shaken together, running over, shall they give into your bosom. For with what measure ye mete it shall be measured to you again" (Luke 6:38, R. V.). The generous man is the mighty man of prayer. The stingy man is the powerless man of prayer.

One of the most wonderful statements about prevailing prayer (already referred to) I John 3:22, "Whatsoever we ask we receive of him, because we keep his commandments, and do those things that are pleasing in his sight," is made in direct connection with generosity toward the needy. In the context we are told that it is when we love, not in word or in tongue, but in deed and in truth, when we open our hearts toward the brother in need, it is then and only then we have confidence toward God in prayer.

Many a man and woman who is seeking to find the secret of their powerlessness in prayer need not seek far; it is nothing more nor less than downright stinginess. George Mueller, to whom reference has already been made, was a mighty man of prayer because he was a mighty giver. What he received from God never stuck to his fingers; he immediately passed it on to others. He was constantly receiving because he was constantly giving. When one thinks of the selfishness of the professing church today, how the orthodox churches of this land do not average one dollar per year per member for foreign missions, it is no wonder that the church has so little power in prayer. If we would get from God we must give to others. Perhaps the most wonderful promise in the Bible in regard to God's supplying our need is Philippians 4:19, "And my God shall fulfill every need of yours according to his riches in glory in Christ Jesus" (R. V.). This glorious promise was made to the Philippian church and made in immediate connection with their generosity.

5.   The fifth hindrance to prayer is found in Mark 11:25, "And when ye stand praying, *forgive,* if ye have

ought against any; that your Father also which is in heaven may forgive you your trespasses."

An unforgiving spirit is one of the commonest hindrances to prayer. Prayer is answered on the basis that our sins are forgiven; but God cannot deal with us on the basis of forgiveness while we are harboring ill will against those who have wronged us. Anyone who is nursing a grudge against another has fast closed the ear of God against his own petition. How many there are crying to God for the conversion of husband, children, friends, and wondering why it is that their prayer is not answered when the whole secret is some grudge that they have in their hearts against someone who has injured them or who they fancy has injured them. Many and many a mother and father are allowing their children to go down to eternity unsaved for the miserable gratification of hating somebody.

6.   The sixth hindrance to prayer is found in I Peter 3:7, "Ye husbands, in like manner, dwell with your wives according to knowledge, giving honor unto the woman, as unto the weaker vessel as being also joint-heirs of the grace of life; to the end that your prayers be not hindered" (R. V.). Here we are plainly told that *a wrong relation between husband and wife is a hindrance to prayer*.

In many and many a case the prayers of husbands are hindered because of their failure of duty toward their wives. On the other hand it is also doubtless true that the prayers of wives are hindered because of their failure in duty toward their husbands. If husbands and wives should seek diligently to find the cause of their unanswered prayers they would often find it in their relations to one another.

Many a man who makes great pretensions to piety and is very active in Christian work shows but little consideration in his treatment of his wife, and is oftentimes unkind, if not brutal; then he wonders why it is that his prayers are not answered. The verse that we have just quoted explains the seeming mystery. On the other hand, many a woman who is very devoted to the church, and very faithful in attendance upon all services treats her husband with the most unpardonable neglect, is cross and peevish toward him, wounds him by the sharpness of her speech and by her ungovernable temper; then wonders why it is that she has no power in prayer.

There are other things in the relations of husbands and wives which cannot be spoken of publicly but which doubtless are oftentimes a hindrance in approaching God in prayer. There is much of sin covered up under the holy name of marriage that is a cause of spiritual deadness and of powerlessness in prayer. Any man or woman whose prayers seem to bring no answer should spread their whole married life out before God and ask Him to put His finger upon anything in it that is displeasing in His sight.

7. The seventh hindrance to prayer is found in James 1:5-7, "But if any of you lacketh wisdom, let him ask of God, who giveth to all liberally and upbraideth not; and it shall be given him. But let him ask *in faith, nothing doubting*: for he that doubteth is like the surge of the sea driven by the wind and tossed. For let not that man think that he shall receive anything of the Lord" (R. V.).

Prayers are hindered by unbelief. God demands that we shall believe His Word absolutely. To question it is to make Him a liar. Many of us do that when we plead His promises and is it any wonder that our prayers are not answered? How many prayers are hindered by our wretched unbelief! We go to God and ask Him for something that is positively promised in His Word and then we do not more than half expect to get it. "Let not that man think that he shall receive anything of the Lord."

CHAPTER 10

WHEN TO PRAY

>>>> If we would know the fullness of blessing that there is in the prayer life it is important not only that we pray in the right way but also that we pray at the right time. Christ's own example is full of suggestiveness as to the right time for prayer.

1.   In the first chapter of Mark, verse 35, we read, "And *in the morning,* rising up *a great while before day,* he went out, and departed into a solitary place, and there prayed."

Jesus chose the early morning hour for prayer. Many of the mightiest men of God have followed the Lord's example in this. In the morning hour the mind is fresh and at its very best. It is free from distraction and that absolute concentration upon God which is essential to the most effective prayer is most easily possible in the early morning hours. Furthermore, when the early hours are spent in prayer the whole day is sanctified and power is obtained for overcoming its temptations and for performing its duties. More can be accomplished in prayer in the first hours of the day than at any other time during the day. Every child of God who would make the most out of his life for Christ should set apart the first part of the day to meeting God in the study of His Word and in prayer. The first thing we do each day should be to go alone with God and face the duties, the temptations, and the service of that day, and get strength from God for all. We should get victory before the hour of trial, temptation or service comes. The secret place of prayer is the place to fight our battles and gain our victories.

2.   In the sixth chapter of Luke, verse 12, we get further light upon the right time to pray. We read, "And it came to pass in those days, and he went out into a mountain to pray, and continued *all night* in prayer to God."

Here we see Jesus praying in the night, spending the entire night in prayer. Of course we have no reason to suppose that this was the constant practice of our Lord nor do we even know how common this practice was, but there were certainly times when the whole night was given up to prayer. Here too we do well to follow in the footsteps of the Master.

Of course there is a way of setting apart nights for prayer in which there is no profit; it is pure legalism. But the abuse of this practice is no reason for neglecting it altogether. One ought not to say, "I am going to spend a whole night in prayer," with the thought that there is any merit that will win God's favor in such an exercise; that is legalism. But we oftentimes do well to say, "I am going to set apart this night for meeting God and obtaining His blessing and power; and if necessary, and if He so leads me, I will give the whole night to prayer." Oftentimes we will have prayed things through long before the night has passed and we can retire and find more refreshing and invigorating sleep than if we had not spent the time in prayer. At other times God doubtless will keep us in communion with Himself away into the morning; and when He does this in His infinite grace, blessed indeed are these hours of night prayer!

Nights of prayer to God are followed by days of power with men. In the night hours the world is hushed in slumber and we can easily be alone with God and have undisturbed communion with Him. If we set apart the whole night for prayer there will be no hurry, there will be time for our own hearts to become quiet before God, there will be time for the whole mind to be brought under the guidance of the Holy Spirit, there will be plenty of time to pray things through. A night of prayer should be put entirely under God's control. We should lay down no rules as to how long we will pray or as to what we shall pray about, but be ready to wait upon God for a short time or a long time as He may lead and to be led out in one direction or another as He may see fit.

3.   Jesus Christ prayed *before all the great crises in His earthly life.*

He prayed before choosing the twelve disciples; before the sermon on the mount; before starting out on an evangelistic tour; before His anointing with the Holy Spirit and His entrance upon His public ministry; before announcing to the Twelve His approaching death; before the great consummation of His life at the cross (Luke 6:12, 13; Luke 9:18, 21, 22; Luke 3:21, 22; Mark 1:35-38; Luke 32:39-46). He prepared for every important crisis by a protracted season of prayer. So ought we to do also. Whenever any crisis of life is seen to be approaching we should prepare for it by a season of very definite prayer to God. We should take plenty of time for this prayer.

4.   Christ prayed not only before the great events and victories of His life, but He also prayed *after its great achievements and important crises.*

When He had fed the five thousand with the five loaves and two fishes and the multitude desired to take Him and make Him king, having sent them away He went up into the mountain apart to pray and spent hours there alone in prayer to God (Matt. 14:23; John 6:15). So He went on from victory to victory.

It is more common for most of us to pray before the great events of life than it is to pray after them but the latter is as important as the former. If we would pray after the great achievements of life we might go on to still greater; as it is we are often either puffed up or exhausted by the things that we do in the name of the Lord and so we advance no further. Many and many a man in answer to prayer has been endued with power and thus has wrought great things in the name of the Lord, and when these great things were accomplished instead of going alone with God and humbling himself before Him and giving Him all the glory for what was achieved he has congratulated himself upon what has been accomplished, has become puffed up, and God has been obliged to lay him aside. The great things done were not followed by humiliation of self, and prayer to God, and so pride has come in and the mighty man has been shorn of his power.

5.   Jesus Christ gave a special time to prayer *when life was unusually busy*. He would withdraw in such a time from the multitudes that thronged about Him and go into the wilderness and pray. For example, we read in Luke 5:15, 16, "But so much the more went abroad the report concerning him and great multitudes came together to hear, and to be healed of their infirmities. But he withdrew himself in the deserts and prayed" (R. V.).

Some men are so busy that they find no time for prayer. Apparently the busier Christ's life was the more He prayed. Sometimes He had no time to eat (Mark 3:20); sometimes He had no time for needed rest and sleep (Mark 6:31, 33, 46); but He always took time to pray; and the more the work crowded the more He prayed.

Many a mighty man of God has learned this secret from Christ. When the work has crowded more than usual they have set an unusual amount of time apart for prayer. Other men of God, once mighty, have lost their power because they did not learn this secret and allowed increasing work to crowd out prayer.

Years ago it was the writer's privilege, with other theological students, to ask questions of one of the most useful Christian men of the day. The writer was led to ask, "Will you tell us something of your prayer life?"

The man was silent a moment, and then, turning his eyes earnestly upon me, replied: "Well, I must admit that I have been so crowded with work of late that I have not given the time I should to prayer."

Is it any wonder that that man lost power and the great work that he was doing was curtailed in a very marked degree? Let us never forget that the more the work presses on us the more time must we spend in prayer.

6.   Jesus Christ prayed *before the great temptations of His life.*

As He drew nearer and nearer to the cross and realized that upon it was to come the great final test of His life, Jesus went out into the garden to pray. He came "unto a place called Gethsemane, and saith unto the disciples, Sit ye here while I go and pray yonder" (Matt. 26:36). The victory of Calvary was won that night in the garden of Gethsemane. The calm majesty of His bearing in meeting the awful onslaughts of Pilate's Judgment Hall and of Calvary was the outcome of the struggle, agony and victory of Gethsemane. While Jesus prayed the disciples slept so He stood fast while they fell ignominiously.

Many temptations come upon us unawares and unannounced and all that we can do is to lift a cry to God for help then and there; but many of the temptations of life we can see approaching from the distance and in such cases the victory should be won before the temptation really reaches us.

7.   In I Thessalonians 5:17 we read, "Pray *without ceasing,*" and in Ephesians 6:18 (R. V.), "Praying *at all seasons.*"

Our whole life should be a life of prayer. We should walk in constant communion with God. There should be a constant upward looking of the soul to God. We should walk so habitually in His presence that even when we awake in the night it would be the most natural thing in the world for us to speak to Him in thanksgiving or in petition.

CHAPTER 11

PRAYER FOR A GENERAL REVIVAL

>>>> If we are to pray aright in such a time as this much of our prayer should be for a general revival. If there was ever a time in which there was need to cry unto God in the words of the Psalmist, "Wilt thou not revive us again, that thy people may rejoice in thee?" (Psa. 85:6), it is this day in which we live. It is surely time for the Lord to work, for men have made void His law (Psa. 119:126). The voice of the Lord given in the written Word is set at naught both by the world and the church. Such a time is not a time for discouragement—the man who believes in God and believes in the Bible can never be discouraged; but it is a time for Jehovah Himself to step in and work.

A revival is a time of quickening or impartation of life. As God alone can give life, a revival is a time when God visits His people and by the power of His Spirit imparts new life to them and through them imparts life to sinners dead in trespasses and sins. *New life from God—*

that is a revival. A general revival is a time when this new life from God is not confined to scattered localities but is general throughout Christendom and the earth.

The reason why a general revival is needed is that spiritual dearth and desolation and death is general. It is not confined to any one country, though it may be more manifest in some countries than in others. It is found in foreign mission fields as well as in home fields.

In times of revival Christians come out from the world and live separated lives. Christians who have been dallying with the world, and indulging in its follies, give them up. These things are found to be incompatible with increasing life and light.

In times of revival Christians get a new spirit of prayer. Prayer meetings are no longer a duty but become the necessity of a hungry, importunate heart. Private prayer is followed with new zest. The voice of earnest prayer to God is heard day and night. People no longer ask, "Does God answer prayer?" They know He does and besiege the throne of grace day and night.

In times of revival Christians go to work for lost souls. They do not go to meeting simply to enjoy themselves and get blessed. They go to meeting to watch for souls and to bring them to Christ. They talk to men on the street and in the stores and in their homes. The cross of Christ, salvation, Heaven and Hell become the subjects of constant conversation. Politics and the weather and new cars and the latest novels are forgotten.

In times of revival Christians have new joy in Christ. Life is joy, and new life is new joy. Revival days are glad days, days of Heaven on earth.

But revivals also have a decided influence on the unsaved world.

First of all, they bring deep conviction of sin. Jesus said that when the Spirit was come He would convince the world of sin (John 16:7, 8). Now we have seen that a revival is a coming of the Holy Spirit, and therefore there must be new conviction of sin, and there always is. If you see something men call a revival and there is no conviction of sin you may know at once that it is bogus. It is a sure mark.

Revivals bring also conversion and regeneration. When God refreshes His people, He always converts sinners also. The first result of Pentecost was new life and power to the one hundred and twenty disciples in the upper room; the second result was three thousand conversions in a single day. It is always so.

Why General Revival Is Needed

We see what a general revival is and what it does; let us now face the question why it is needed at the present time.

Look at the spiritual state of the church. Worldliness is rampant among church members. Many church members are just as eager as any in the rush to get rich. They use the methods of the world in the accumulation of wealth and they hold just as fast to it as any when they have gotten it.

Prayerlessness abounds among church members on every hand. Someone has said that Christians on the average do not spend more than five minutes a day in prayer.

Neglect of the Word of God goes hand in hand with neglect of prayer to God. Very many Christians spend twice as much time every day wallowing through the mire of the daily papers as they do bathing in the cleansing laver of God's Holy Word.

Along with neglect of prayer and neglect of the Word of God goes a lack of generosity. The churches are rapidly increasing in wealth, but the treasuries of the missionary societies are empty. Christians do not average a dollar a year for foreign missions. It is appalling.

Christians mingle with the world in all forms of questionable amusements. The young man or young woman who does not believe in dancing with its rank immodesties, in the card table with its drift toward gambling, and in the theater with its ever increasing appeal to lewdness, is counted an old fogey.

Then how small a proportion of our membership has really entered into fellowship with Jesus Christ in His burden for souls! Enough has been said of the spiritual state of the church.

3. Now look at the state of the world.

There is lack of conviction of sin. Seldom are men overwhelmed with a sense of their awful guilt in trampling under foot the Son of God. Sin is regarded as a "misfortune" or as "infirmity," or even as "good in the making"; seldom as enormous wrong against a holy God.

Unbelief is rampant. Many regard it as a mark of intellectual superiority to reject the Bible, and even faith in God and immortality. It is about the only mark of intellectual superiority many possess, and perhaps that is the reason they cling to it so tenaciously.

Hand in hand with this widespread infidelity goes gross immorality, as has always been the case. Infidelity and immorality are Siamese twins. They always exist and always grow and always fatten together. This prevailing immorality is found everywhere.

Greed for money has become a mania with rich and poor. The multimillionaire will often sell his soul and trample the rights of his fellow men under foot in the mad hope of becoming a billionaire and the laboring man will often commit murder to increase the power of the union and keep up wages. Wars are waged and men shot down like dogs to improve commerce and to gain political prestige for unprincipled politicians who parade as statesmen.

The licentiousness of the day lifts its serpent head everywhere. You see it in the newspapers, you see it on the billboards. You see it on the streets at night. You see it just outside the church door. You find it not only in the awful cesspools set apart for it in the great cities, but it is crowding further and further up our business streets and into the residence portions of our cities. The moral condition of the world in our day is disgusting, sickening, appalling.

We need a revival, deep, widespread, general, in the power of the Holy Ghost. It is either a general revival or the dissolution of the church, of the home, of the state. A revival, new life from God, is the cure, and the only cure. That will stem the awful tide of immorality and unbelief. Mere argument will not do it; but a wind from Heaven, a new outpouring of the Holy Ghost, a true God-sent revival will.

The need is clear. What then shall we do? Pray. Take up the Psalmist's prayer, "Revive us again, that thy people may rejoice in thee." Take up Ezekiel's prayer, "Come from the four winds, O breath [breath of God], and breathe upon these slain that they may live." Hark, I hear a noise!

Behold a shaking! I can almost feel the breeze upon my cheek. I can almost see the great living army rising to their feet. Shall we not pray and pray and pray and pray, till the Spirit moves and God revives His people?